Animal Peculiarity Volume 2 Part 2

By T.P Just

~~~

Copyright © 2012 by T.P Just. All rights reserved.

All Rights Reserved. No part of this publication may be reproduced in any form or by any means, including scanning, photocopying, or otherwise without prior written permission of the copyright holder.

This eBook is licensed for your personal enjoyment only. This eBook may not be re-sold or given away to other people. If you would like to share this book with another person, please purchase an additional copy for each recipientGet All The Books In The Series:

Animal Peculiarity Volume 1 [1-8]
Animal Peculiarity Volume 2 [1-8]
Just Enterprises

I0436332

Table of Contents

1 Prologue

THERE is perhaps nothing extraordinary in the fact that man is wise and just, takes great care to provide for his own children, -shows due consideration for his parents, seeks sustenance for himself, protects himself against plots, and possesses all the other gifts of nature which are his. For man has been endowed with speech, of all things the most precious, and has been granted reason, which is of the greatest help and use.

Moreover, he knows how to reverence and worship the gods. But that dumb animals should by nature possess some good quality and should have many of man's amazing excellences assigned to them along with man, is indeed a remarkable fact. And to know accurately the special characteristics of each, and how living creatures also have been a source of interest no less than man, demands a trained intelligence and much learning. Now I am well aware of the labour that others have expended on this subject, yet I have collected all the materials that I could; I have clothed them in untechnical language, and am persuaded that my achievement is a treasure far from negligible. So if anyone considers them profitable, let him make use of them; anyone who does not consider them so may give them to his father to keep and attend to.

For not all things give pleasure to all men, nor do all men consider all subjects worthy of study. Although I was born later than many accomplished writers of an earlier day, the accident of date ought not to mulct me of praise, if I too produce a learned work whose ampler research and whose choice of language make it deserving of serious attention.

2 Elephants worship in the moon

I am informed that when the new moon begins to appear, Elephants by some natural and un- explained act of intelligence pluck fresh branches from the forest where they feed and then raise them aloft and look upwards at the goddess, waving the branches gently to and fro, as though they were offering her in a sense a suppliants olive-branch in the hope that she will prove kindly and benevolent to them.

The Mare

I have heard that Mares are the only animals which when pregnant allow the male to have inter-course with them. For Mares are exceedingly lustful, and that is why strict censors call lecherous women 'mares.

The Partridge, it's young Partridges while still in the egg and confined by the shell that has formed around them do not wait for their parents to hatch them out, but alone and unaided, like house-breakers, peck through the eggs, peep out, and then lever themselves up, and then after cracking the egg-shell begin at once to run. And if half the shell is clinging to their tail they shake it off and cast it from them; and they hunt for food and dart about at great speed.

The Partridge-three kinds

Partridges that utter clear, musical tones are confident in their vocal skill. So too the fighting birds which compete feel certain that when captured they will not be regarded as merely fit for sacrifice.

And that is why when caught they struggle less against their pursuers in order to avoid capture. But the rest, and especially the Partridges of Cirrha, conscious that they possess neither strength nor ability to sing, and knowing full well that if caught they will furnish a meal for their captors; do their utmost, prompted by some natural intelligence, to render themselves unfit for eating.

And they abstain from other food which delights and fattens them and feed most eagerly upon garlic. Hence those who are already aware of these facts have willingly agreed that they should be immune from pursuit. Whereas a man who has not previously chanced to hunt them, if he catches and cooks them, has wasted» his time and his pains over them, when he finds their flesh disgusting.

3 The Wolf, when full-fed

The Wolf when gorged to satiety will not thereafter taste the least morsel. For his belly is distended, his tongue swells, his mouth is blocked, and he is gentle as a lamb to meet, and would have no designs on man or beast, even were he to walk through the middle of a flock.

Gradually however and little by little his tongue shrinks and resumes its former shape, and he becomes once more a wolf.

Marten and Snake

The Marten is an evil creature, and an evil creature is the Snake. And so when a Marten means to fight with a Snake, it chews some rue beforehand and then goes out boldly to battle, as though fortified and armed. The reason is that to a Snake rue is utterly abhorrent.

4 The Partridge as decoy-bird

Cockerels all tread a newcomer to the flock, and tame
Partridges do the same to the latest arrival as yet untamed.
And Partridges even requite their own parents by decoying
those that are free and wild, acting in this respect just like
pigeons.

Now this is the way in which the Partridge draws them to him
and displays the arts of a Siren to allure others. He stands
uttering his cry, and his tune conveys a challenge, provoking
the wild bird to fight; and he stands in ambush by the spring.

Then the cock of the wild birds answers back and advances to
do battle on behalf of his covey. So the tame bird withdraws,
pretending to be afraid, while the other advances vaunting as
though he were already victorious, is caught in the snare, and
is captured.

Now if it is a cock bird that falls into the trap, his companions
attempt to bring help to the captive; but if it is a hen, one here
and another there beats the captive for allowing her lust to
bring her into slavery.

And here is a point that I will not omit, for it deserves attention. If the decoy-bird is a hen, the wild hens, in order to prevent the cock from falling into the trap, counter the challenge with their cries and rescue the cock that is about to be trapped, for he is glad to stay with those who are his mates and more numerous, seeming to be drawn by some spell that is in truth love

5 The Lynx

The Lynx

The Lynx hides its urine, for when it hardens it turns to stone and is suitable for engraving, and is one of the aids to female adornment, so they say.

The Hedgehog

The Hedgehog too is believed to be one of the animals that show spite. Thus, when it is caught it immediately makes water on its skin, so rendering it unfit for use, though it is thought to serve many purposes.

Objects poisonous to certain animals

If a Lion eats a Lion's-bane it dies. And insects are destroyed if one drops oil on them. And perfumes are the death of Vultures. Beetles you will extirpate if you scatter roses on them.

The Indian Hound

The Hounds of India are reckoned as wild animals; they are exceedingly strong and fierce- tempered, and are the largest dogs in the world. All other animals they despise; but an Indian Hound will engage with a lion and resist its onslaught, barking against its roar and giving bite for bite.

Only after much worrying and wounding of the lion is the Hound finally overcome; and even a lion might be overcome by an Indian Hound, for once it has bitten, the Hound holds fast. And even if you take a sword and cut off a Hound's leg, it has no thought, in spite of its pain, of relaxing its bite, but though its leg has been cut off, only when dead does it let go and lie still, forced by death to desist.

What more I have learned I will recount elsewhere.

Peculiarities of various creatures

Men and Dogs are the only creatures that belch after they have eaten their fill. A man's heart is attached to his left breast, but in other creatures it is fixed in the centre of the thorax. Among birds of prey there is not one that drinks or makes water, or even gathers in flocks with others of its kind. There is in India. a wild beast, powerful, daring, as big as the largest lion, of a red colour like cinnabar, shaggy like a dog, and in the language of India it is called Martich0ms.l' Its face however is not that of a wild beast but of a man, and it has three rows of teeth set in its upper jaw and three in the lower; these are exceedingly sharp and larger than the fangs of a. hound.

Its ears also resemble a man's, except that they are larger and shaggy; its eyes are blue-grey and they too are like a man's, but its feet and claws, you must know, are those of a lion. To the end of its tail is attached the sting of a scorpion, and this might be over a cubit in length; and the tail has stings at intervals on either side. But the tip of the tail gives a fatal sting to anyone who encounters it, and death is immediate.

If one pursues the beast it lets fly its stings, like arrows, sideways, and it can shoot a great distance; and when it discharges its stings straight ahead it bends its tail back; if how- ever it shoots in a backward direction, as the Sacae do, then it stretches its tail to its full extent. Any creature that the missile hits it kills; the elephant alone it does not kill.

These stings which it shoots are a foot long and the thickness of a bulrush. Now Ctesias asserts (and he says that the Indians confirm his words) that in the places where those stings have been let fly others spring up, so that this evil produces a crop. And according to the same writer the Manti chore for choice devours human beings; indeed it will slaughter a great number; and it lies in wait not for a single man but would set upon two or even three men, and alone overcomes even that number. All other animals it defeats: the lion alone it can never bring down.

That this creature takes special delight in gorging human flesh its very name testifies, for in the Greek language it means man-eater, and its name is derived from its activities. Like the stag it is extremely swift.

Now the Indians hunt the young of these animals while they are still without stings in their tails, which they then crush with a stone to prevent them from growing stings. The sound of their voice is as near as possible that of a trumpet.

Ctesias declares that he has actually seen this animal in Persia (it had been brought from India as a present to the Persian King)-if Ctesias is to be regarded as a sufficient authority on such matters.

At any rate after hearing of the peculiarities of this animal, one must pay heed to the historian of Cnidos.

The power of human spittle

The Sea-scolopendra bursts, they say, when a man spits in its face.

The Willow

If one crushes the fruit of a Willow-tree and gives it to animals to drink, they suffer no injury at all, and rather they thrive on it.

But if a man drinks it, his semen loses its pro creative strength. And I fancy that Homer had explored the secrets of nature when he wrote in his verses 'and willows that lose their fruit,' and that he was making a cryptic allusion to this.

Hemlock

And if a man drink Hemlock, he dies from the congealing and chilling of his blood, whereas a hog can gorge itself with Hemlock and remain in good health.

7 Oxen treading out the corn

In the threshing season when the oxen move round the threshing-floor and the space is filled with sheaves, in order to prevent the oxen from eating the ears, the men smear their nostrils with dung-a device which they have hit upon and which serves them well.

For this animal is so disgusted at the aforesaid smearing that it would not touch any food, even though it were assailed with the fiercest hunger.

The taming of Elephants

The Indians have difficulty in capturing a full-grown Elephant. So they resort to the swamps by a river and then capture the young ones. For the Elephant delights in moist places where the ground is soft, and loves the water, and prefers to pass his time in these haunts: he is, so to say, a creature of the swamps.

So having caught them while tender and docile, they look after them, pandering to their appetites, grooming their bodies, and using soothing words-for the Elephants understand the speech of the natives-and, in a word, they foster them like children and bestow care upon them, instructing them in various ways. And the baby Elephants learn to obey.

8 Falconry in India

This is the way in which the Indians hunt Hares and Foxes: they have no need of hounds for the chase, but they catch the young of Eagles, Ravens, and Kites also, rear them, and teach them how to hunt.

This is their method of instruction: to a tame Hare or to a domesticated Fox they attach a piece of meat, and then let them run; and having sent the birds in pursuit, they allow them to pick off the meat.

The birds give chase at full speed, and if they catch the Hare or the Fox, they have the meat as a reward for the capture: it is for them highly attractive bait.

When therefore they have perfected the birds' skill at hunting, the Indians let them loose after mountain Hares and wild Foxes.

And the birds, in expectation of their accustomed feed, whenever one of these animals appears, fly after it, seize it in a trice, and bring it back to their masters, as Ctesias tells us.

And from the same source we learn also that in place of the meat which has hitherto been attached, the entrails of the animals they have caught provide a meal.

9 The Gryphons and the gold of Bactria

I have heard that the Indian animal the Gryphon is a quadruped like a lion; that it has claws of enormous strength and that they resemble those of a lion. Men commonly report that it is winged and that the feathers along its back are black, and those on its front are red, while the actual wings are neither but are white.

And Ctesias records that its neck is variegated with feathers of a dark blue; that it has a beak like an eagle's, and a head too, just as artists portray it in pictures and sculpture. Its eyes, he says, are like fire. It builds its lair among the mountains, and although it is not possible to capture the full-grown animal, they do take the young ones.

And the people of Bactria, who are neighbors of the Indians, say that the Gryphons guard the gold in those parts; that they dig it up and build their nests with it, and that the Indians carry off any that falls from them.

The Indians however deny that they guard the aforesaid gold, for the Gryphons have no need of it (and if that is what they say, then I at any rated think that they speak the truth), but that they themselves come to collect the gold, While the Gryphons fearing for their young ones fight with the invaders. They engage too with other beasts and overcome them without difficulty, but they will not face the lion or the elephant. Accordingly the natives, dreading the strength of these animals, do not set out in quest of the gold by day, but arrive by night, for at that season they are less likely to be detected.

Now the region where the Gryphons live and where the gold is mined is a dreary wilderness.

And the seekers after the aforesaid substance arrive, a thousand or two strong, armed and bringing spades and sacks; and watching for a moonless night they begin to dig. Now if they contrive to elude the Gryphons they reap a double advantage, for they not only escape with their lives but they also take home their freight, and when those who have acquired a special skill in the smelting of gold have refined it, they possess immense wealth to requite them for the dangers described above. If however they are caught in the act, they are lost. And they return home, I am told, after an interval of three or four years.

10 The Turtle and its eyes

The head of a Turtle, after it has been cut off sees and closes its eyes if one brings one's hand near; and it would still 'bite if you brought your hand too near.

It has eyes that flash a long way off, for the pupils are the purest white and very conspicuous, and when removed are set in gold and necklaces. For that reason they are greatly admired by women. These Turtles, I learn, are natives of what is commonly called the 'Red Sea.'

11 The Cock and its crowing

The Cock, they say, at moon rise becomes possessed and jumps about. Never would a sunrise pass unnoticed by him, but at that hour he excels himself in crowing. And I learn that the Cock is the favourite bird of Leto.

The reason is, they say, that he was at her side when she was so happily brought to bed of twins. That is why to this very day a Cock is at hand when women are in travail, and is believed somehow to promote an easy delivery.

If the Hen dies the Cock himself sits on the eggs and hatches his own eggs in silence, for then for some strange and inexplicable reason, I must say, he does not crow. I fancy that he is conscious that he is then doing the work of a female and not of a male.

A Cock that has been defeated in battle and in at struggle with another will not crow, for his spirit is depressed and he hides himself in shame. On the other hand if he is victorious, he is proud and holds his head high and appears exultant.

Here too is a most astonishing trait, I think. As he passes beneath a doorway, no matter how high, the Cock lowers his head-a most pretentious action, done apparently to protect his comb.

12 The Jackdaw

Jackdaws are devoted to their own species; and this it is that often causes their destruction. And it happens in this way. The man who intends to hunt Jackdaws adopts the following plan.

How caught

In the place where he knows that they feed and where he sees them gathering in flocks he arranges basins full of oil.
Now the oil is transparent and the bird is inquisitive, and it comes and perches on the rim of the vessel, bends down, and sees its own reflection, and supposing it to be another Jackdaw, makes haste to go down to it.
So it descends, flaps its wings, and scatters the oil all over itself. Being quite unable to fly up again the bird remains, so to speak, fettered, though neither net nor trap nor snare is there.

13 The Elephant, its anatomy and habits

The Elephant has what some call protruding tusks, what others call horns. On each foot he has five toes; their growth is just visible although they are not separate; and that is why he is ill-adapted for swimming.

His hind legs are shorter than his fore-legs; his paps are close to his armpits: he has a proboscis which is far more serviceable than a hand, and his tongue is short; his gall-bladder is said to be not near the liver but close to the intestines

I am informed that the duration of the Elephant's pregnancy is two years; although others maintain that it is not so long, but only eighteen months. It bears a young one as big as a one-year-old calf, which pulls at the dug with its mouth.

When it is possessed with a desire to copulate and is burning with passion, it will dash at a wall and overturn it, will bend palm- trees by butting its forehead against them, as rams do. It drinks water not when clear and pure but when it has dirtied and stirred it up a little.

But it sleeps standing upright, for it finds the act of lying down and of rising troublesome. The Elephant reaches its prime at the age of sixty, though its life extends to two hundred years. But it cannot endure cold.

14 The Goats and Sheep of India

It is worth while learning the nature of the locks that belong to the Indians. I have heard that their Goats and their Sheep are larger than the largest asses, and that each one gives birth to quadruplets; anyhow no Goat or Sheep in India would ever give birth to less than three at a time.

The Sheep have tails reaching down to their feet, while the Goats have tails of such length as all but touch the ground. The shepherds cut off the tails of the ewes which are good for breeding so that the rams may mount them, and they press oil 'out of the fat contained in them. In the rams' tails also they make an incision and extract the fat and sew them up again. And the cut joins up once more and all traces of it disappear.

The Chameleon and Snakes

Alexander of Myndus declares that the Chameleon annoys snakes and makes them go hungry in this way. Taking in its teeth a piece of wood, broad and solid, it turns about and goes to face its enemy.

But the Snake is unable to seize it as its jaws cannot compass the width of the wood; and so the Snake goes without a meal as far as the Chameleon is concerned, for-although it may bite the rest of its body it gains nothing, since the Chameleon has a solid hide and cares not at all for the fangs of the Snake.

15 The Lion

The neck of a Lion consists of a single bone and not of a number of vertebrae. And if a man cuts through the bones of a Lion, fire leaps forth. But they are devoid of marrow, nor are they hollow like tubes.

There is no season of the year in which it abstains from coupling, and the Lioness is pregnant for two months. Five times does she give birth, at the first birth to five cubs, at the second to four, after that to three, after that to two, and finally to one.

The cubs when newborn are small and, like puppies, blind, "and they begin to walk when they have completed two months from birth. But the account which says that they scratch through the womb is a fable.

To encounter a Lion when famished is dangerous, but when he has eaten his fill he is extremely gentle; they even say that at that time he is playful. A Lion will never turn his back and flee, but withdraws, looking you straight in the face, and by degrees.

But when he begins to age he visits folds and huts and spots where shepherds lodge in caves; which, is to be expected, because he no longer has the spirit for hunting on the mountains. He has a horror of fire.

Any Lion that inclines to roundness and a compact figure, and that has too shaggy a mane, appears to be lacking in spirit and daring; whereas the beast that attains a good length and has a straight mane is regarded as bolder and fiercer.

Possessing a ravenous appetite he will, they say, devour and swallow whole limbs. So when he has taken his fill of them he will often not eat for the space of three days until his former meal has been gradually absorbed and digested. He drinks but little.

16 The Purple Snake of India

Historians say that India is rich in drugs and remarkably prolific of medicinal plants, of which some save life and rescue from danger men who have been brought to death's door through the bites of noxious creatures (and there are many such in India)

While other drugs are swift to kill and destroy; and to this class might be assigned the drug which comes from the Purple Snake. Now this snake appears to be a span long; its colour is like the deepest purple, but its head they describe as white and not purple, and not just white, but whiter even than snow or milk.

But this snake has no fangs and is found in the hottest regions of India, and though it is quite incapable of biting-for which reason you might pronounce it to be tame and gentle-yet if it vomits upon anyone (so I am told), be it man or animal, the entire limb inevitably putrefies.

Therefore when caught men hang it up by the tail, and naturally it has its head hanging down, looking at the ground. And below the creature's mouth they place a bronze vessel, into which there ooze drops from its mouth; and the liquid sets and congeals, and if you saw it you would say that it was gum from an almond-tree

So when the snake is dead they remove the vessel and substitute another, also of bronze; and again from the dead body there flows a liquid serum which looks like water. This they leave for three days, and it too sets; but there will be a difference in colour between the two, for the latter is a deep black and the former the colour of amber.

Now if you give a man a piece of this no bigger than a sesame seed, dropping it into his Wine or his food, first he will be seized with convulsions of the utmost violence; next, his eyes squint and his brain dissolves and drips through his nostrils, and he dies a most pitiable death. And if he takes a smaller dose of the poison, there is no escape for him hereafter, for in time he dies.

If however you administer some of the black matter which has flowed from the snake when dead, again a piece the size of a sesame seed, the man's body begins to suppurate, a wasting sickness overtakes him, and within a year he is carried off by consumption.

But there are many whose lives have been prolonged for as much as two years, while little by little they died.

17 The Ostrich

Although the Ostrich lays a number of eggs it does not hatch all of them but sets aside the sterile ones and sits upon those that are fertile; and from these it hatches its young, giving them the other, rejected eggs to eat.

And if one chases the Ostrich it does not venture to fly but spreads its wings and runs. And if it is in danger of being captured it slings the stones that come in its way, backwards with its feet.

The Sparrow

Sparrows, conscious that their weakness is due to the small size of their bodies, build their nests upon those twigs of branches which are strong enough to support them, and so generally escape the machinations of bird-catchers who cannot climb the branch: it is too slender to bear them.

18 The Fox and Wasps

Foxes pass a pound in their mischievousness and trickery.
When they observe a thriving Wasps nest they turn their back
upon it and avoid the hole so as to protect themselves from
being stung.

But their tail, which is very bushy and long, they let down into
the hole and shake up the Wasps. And these fasten on the
thick hairs. But when they are entangled in them the Foxes
beat their tail against la tree or fence or stone wall, and the
Wasps are killed by the blows.

Then the Foxes return to the same spot, collect the remaining
Wasps, and kill them as they did the first lot. When they know
that they will have peace and be free from stings they put
down their heads and eat up the combs, with nothing to
disturb them and no need to look out for stings.

The Dog

A Dog's skull has no suture. Running they say, makes a Dog more lustful. In old age a Dog's teeth are blunt and turn black. He is so keen- scented that he will never touch the roasted flesh of a dog, be it bewitched by the subtlest and craftiest of rich sauces.

Now there are three diseases which fall to the lot of a Dog and no more, viz. dog-quinsy, rabies, and gout, while mankind has an infinite number. Everything that is bitten by a mad Dog dies.

If a Dog once gets gout you will hardly see him recover his strength. The life of a Dog at its longest is-fourteen years; so Argus, the dog of Odysseus, and the story about him.

Get All The Books In The Series:

www.ingramcontent.com/pod-product-compliance
Lightning Source LLC
Chambersburg PA
CBHW050905290526
45792CB00002B/717